Sham
(The Shining Star)

Helps Daniel from the Lyin' Den

Written by
Joyce J. Ashley

Illustrated by
Jamie Ashley

Copyright © 2015 by Joyce J. Ashley Jamie Ashley, Illustrator

SHAMGAR (THE SHINING STAR)
Helps Daniel From The Lyin' Den
by Joyce J. Ashley Jamie Ashley, Illustrator

Printed in the United States of America

ISBN 9781498453059

All rights reserved solely by the author. The author guarantees all contents are original and do not infringe upon the legal rights of any other person or work. No part of this book may be reproduced in any form without the permission of the author. The views expressed in this book are not necessarily those of the publisher.

Scripture.quotations taken from the Holy Bible, New International Version (NIV). Copyright © 1973, 1978, 1984, 2011 by Biblica, Inc.™. Used by permission. All rights reserved.

www.xulonpress.com

Presented to...

_____

With much love and joy from...

_____

On

_____

PREFACE

SHAMGAR (The Shining Star) was inspired by Dr. Jay Strack and Pat Williams through their book entitled, <u>The Three Success Secrets of Shamgar.</u> In their book, the authors motivate others to use their ordinary abilities to accomplish extraordinary things. How? By placing trust in God and using "three secrets".

Shamgar, an obscure man from the Bible, is their example. Through our limited knowledge of his life, we can gain much wisdom. As the third judge of Israel, Shamgar slew six hundred Philistines--with an ox goad! Not a sword or a spear or even a bow & arrows! His weapon was a simple ox goad...a strong, crude stick about eight feet long which was primarily used to prod oxen while plowing the fields.

There are only two verses in the Bible about Shamgar: Judges 3:31 and Judges 5:6. Because of his determination to "start where he was, use what he had and do what he could", Shamgar saved Israel. One person CAN make a difference! Though he lived more than 3,000 years ago, the truths drawn from Shamgar's example are still applicable today.

The three "secrets" from Mr. Williams' and Dr. Strack's book are simple, yet, powerfully life-changing. They are elementary enough for children to understand, recall and apply; they are, also, important enough for adults to use in their daily lives to make a positive difference.

Our world today offers many negative influences. It is the author's desire to share Shamgar's secrets with young readers in such a way that they can remember and apply them consistently. May we partner together as we strive to make a positive difference in our world. God's *best* can be accomplished if you:

- **Start where you are.**
- **Use what you have.**
- **Do what you can.**

In this children's book series, Shamgar is portrayed as a young boy who strives to use his "secrets" in his own life and who teaches them to others. When Biblical principles are instilled in our youth, they will "shine like stars" as Paul encourages us to do in Philippians 2:15. Thus the name, **SHAMGAR (The Shining Star).**

Joyce J. Ashley

DEDICATION

To Dr. Jay Strack: Thank you for sharing Shamgar's "secrets" with countless young people throughout the years. Student Leadership University and your personal example have been a positive influence on thousands. One of those teenagers was our daughter, Alison, who continues to use the principles taught and modeled by you. Thank you for being a "Shamgar"!

To Pat Williams: Though we have never personally met, your influence has touched our family, as well as many others. Indeed, you have exemplified Shamgar's secrets as you lead, teach and inspire others to make a difference.

To my former students: Each one of you holds a special place in my heart. I had you in mind when I wrote this book. Your teacher still loves you!

To my grandjoys: You make the joy of reading even more special. My prayer for each of you is that you will grow into a strong "Shamgar" who will make a difference in this world as you shine for Jesus.

To my husband & best friend: Pat, thank you for always being an encouragement to me in my passionate pursuits and for truly making a positive difference in our entire family. I thank God for such a wonderful life-mate. You are "my Shamgar"!

(Dr. Jay Strack is a dynamic communicator and author. As President and Founder of Student Leadership University, he has inspired and empowered countless young people to be equipped with Christian leadership skills. Pat Williams is senior VP of NBA's Orlando Magic. He is one of America's top motivational speakers and has authored more than 71 books.)

"Come inside, boys, before you get wet!" called Daniel's mother. Shamgar had been invited to his best friend's house to play. It had started to rain, so he and Daniel had to move indoors.

After a snack of juice and cookies in the kitchen, the boys strolled into the den and tried to think of fun indoor games to play.

They played "Guess Which Hand?", but they quickly tired of that. "Hide and Seek" was fun for a while, but the house was small, so they soon ran out of places to hide.

They made up their own game of "Pin the Tail on the Doggie". Daniel's puppy, Jehoshaphat, scampered out of the room and hid under the bed until the coast was clear.

Shamgar and Daniel sat in the floor, bored and gloomy. "Oh, why did it have to rain today?" they asked at exactly the same time! They could be doing lots of fun things outside!

All of a sudden, Daniel's face brightened. "Hey, Sham! I've got it! Grandpa gave me a new ball for my birthday. We could toss it to each other in the den."

"I don't know if that's a good idea, Daniel," cautioned Shamgar. "Your mom might not like us throwing the ball indoors. My parents have a rule at my house that we don't throw things inside."

"Yeah, we do, too," Daniel responded in a hushed voice. "But we'll be very careful. Besides--Mom will never know."

Before Shamgar knew what was happening, Daniel picked up the ball and threw it in his direction. Shamgar jerked his hands up to try to catch it, but the ball took a curve. Instead of heading toward Daniel's outstretched hands, it went straight for Mom's favorite lamp!

CRASH!!!! The lamp hit the floor and broke into what seemed to be a zillion pieces! Shamgar's eyes widened and Daniel's face froze in a look of panic.

"What will we tell Mom?" Daniel's voice shook with dread. "We can't tell her we were throwing the ball in the house. I'll get punished for breaking our family rule!"

Shamgar shook his head. "Daniel, you know you've got to…" (He was going to say "tell the truth" but Daniel interrupted to share his plan.)

"Okay, this is what we'll do," he whispered. "When Mom comes in, we'll say that the window was open and a big gust of wind blew the lamp off the table and it broke."

Shamgar could not believe his ears! Daniel—his BEST friend—was going to tell his mom a story, a fib, an out-and-out lie! He felt guilty about even thinking the word "lie" because that was an ugly word at his house. Both boys had been taught to tell the truth.

Shamgar decided that now would be a good time to practice three "secrets" he had learned and to teach them to his friend, as well.

"No, Daniel," Shamgar said boldly. "We can't tell your mom a lie. Let me tell you three 'secrets' that I learned from my grandparents. My Papa says these 'secrets' work in every situation to help us make the right choice."

"The First Secret: **Start where you are**. We've made a mistake. The lamp is broken. It's like Humpty Dumpty—it can't be put back together again! Let's accept that fact."

"The Second Secret: **Use what you have**. Our parents have taught us to always tell the truth…even if we think we'll get in trouble. That's called honesty. My Gigi says, 'Tell the truth from the start, and you'll find joy in your heart.' "

"The Third Secret: **Do what you can.** Daniel, we've got to tell your Mom exactly what happened; we should admit we made a mistake. Let's apologize and offer to work to pay for the broken lamp."

About that time, the boys heard Mom's footsteps. As she entered the room, she immediately noticed the broken lamp lying on the floor.

"Danieeeellllllllllll......would you like to tell me what happened here?" Mom did not look happy.

Daniel glanced over at Shamgar, then back at his mom. He had an important decision to make. Should he lie to avoid punishment…or should he use Shamgar's "secrets"? Sham said telling the truth was the best way.

Daniel dropped his head, scuffed the toe of his shoe on the floor, took a deep breath and said, "I did it, Mom. I threw my new birthday ball and it knocked over your lamp. I didn't mean to break it. I was trying to toss it to Sham. I am so sorry. I'll work and earn money to buy you new one."

Mom's expression softened.

"Daniel, I am proud of you," she said with a sweet smile. "I know it was tempting to tell a lie about what really happened, but you chose to tell the truth. That's always best! Yes, you must suffer the consequences of making a wrong choice. You disobeyed the 'no throwing inside' rule; **but** you are in a lot less trouble because you told the truth about it. Now, come here and give me a hug!"

the 3 Secrets:

#1 Start where you are.

#2 Use what you have.

#3 Do what you can.

Wow! Daniel couldn't believe how much better he felt as Mom wrapped her arms around him. Telling the truth and being forgiven felt wonderful. Shamgar's "secrets" had really worked! Daniel smiled to himself and vowed never to forget those secrets:

1. Start where you are.
2. Use what you have.
3. Do what you can.

"Hey, guys, look! The rain has stopped and the sun is shining," announced Mom as she loosened her hug.

"Come on, Sham. Let's go outside and play!" Daniel grabbed his new ball and ran toward the door.

"Okay, but don't you think we need to help your mom clean up the broken lamp before we go?" suggested Shamgar.

Daniel nodded; and as they picked up the pieces together, Daniel realized that Shamgar had used his "secrets" again. Daniel was glad that Sham was his best friend!

SHAMGAR
(The Shining Star)

Helps Daniel from the Lyin' Den

Though Shamgar was a true Biblical character who lived more than 3000 years ago, he is still a shining example of how each of us can make good, daily choices. In this colorful book, the "modern day" Shamgar will share secrets that help his readers to make wise choices that will lead them to "shine like stars"! (Philippians 2:15)

Children bring much joy to author, Joyce Ashley. For many years she taught school and served as School Counselor to primary and elementary school students. She and her husband of 43 years, Patrick, have three adult children, two daughters-in-love and six grandjoys (with whom she especially loves reading)! The completion of this book brings Joyce a personal joy of seeing a life-long dream come to fruition. Her love for God and passion for children are the motivation for this first book in the Shamgar series.

Joyce is the founder of JoyJoy Ministries. She has a daily radio program called Joy Juice and has authored three books about joy. As a speaker, writer and a grandmother (Gigi), her heart's desire is to share with others the "inexpressible, glorious joy" (1 Peter 1:8 NIV) which comes from a personal relationship with Christ.

www.joyjoyministries.com

Jamie Ashley fell in love with illustration as a child through her favorite children's books and began creating her own stories and characters early on. After studying art in college and teaching art for several years she is once again illustrating stories and working in a variety of media. Jamie resides in the Atlanta area with her husband, Michael and their two daughters.